Before
They Were
Stars

Before They Were Stars

by John Smallwood

SCHOLASTIC INC.
New York   Toronto   London   Auckland   Sydney
Mexico City   New Delhi   Hong Kong   Buenos Aires

Photo Credits: Unless otherwise noted, all photos are copyright NBA, credit NBAE/Getty Images. Cover: Childhood photographs courtesy of the families; (Clockwise from upper right) Baron Davis: Nick Hura; Mike Bibby: Sam Forencich; Wally Szczerbiak: David Sherman. Intro: Childhood photo courtesy of Tia and Lisa Davis; p. 5: Fernando Medina. Chapter 1: Childhood photos courtesy of the Battier family; Page 8: David Sherman Chapter 2: Childhood photos courtesy of Virginia Bibby; Page 11: Rocky Widner. Chapter 3: Childhood photos courtesy of Portia and Paul Collins; Page 15 (top): Noren Trotman; (bottom): Scott Cunningham. Chapter 4: Childhood photos courtesy of Tia and Lisa Davis; Page 18: Ron Hoskins. Chapter 5: Childhood photos courtesy of Pam Long; Page 22: Allen Einstein. Chapter 6: Childhood photos courtesy of Anne Kidd; Page 29: Andrew Gombert. Chapter 7: Childhood photos courtesy of Helen Mashburn; Page 32: Catherine Steenkeste. Chapter 8: Childhood photos courtesy of Marilyn Sczczerbiak; Page 36: Lisa Blumenfeld; Pages 37–38: Childhood photos courtesy of the families. Page 37 (left): Jose Murphy; (right): Allen Einstein; Page 38 (top left): Gregory Shamus; (top left): Al Bello; (bottom): Catherine Steenkeste. Photo Insert: Page 23: Jarron Collins: Kent Horner; Shane Battier: Catherine Steenkeste; Richard Hamilton: Jesse D. Garrabrant; Page 24: Jamal Mashburn: Layne Murdoch; Baron Davis: Jesse D. Garrabrant; Page 25: Wally Szczerbiak: David Sherman; Mike Bibby: Glenn James; Page 26: Jason Collins: Nathaniel S. Butler; Jason Kidd: Jesse D. Garrabrant

ISBN 0-439-57970-8

12 11 10 9 8 7 6 5 4 3 2 1   3 4 5 6 7 8/0

Printed in the U.S.A.
First Scholastic printing, November 2003
Book Design: Louise Bova
Special thanks to: NBA Player & Talent Relations: Leah Wilcox, Janice Jackson, Wilfred Kirkaldy, and NBA Entertainment & Player Marketing: Charles Rosenzweig.

Introduction

Sometimes NBA players seem like they are larger than life. They are some of the best athletes in the world. But before these players turned into superstars, they were kids — just like you.

What were their lives like when they were kids? How did they get started playing basketball? And how did they make their NBA dreams come true?

This is your chance to find out exactly what growing up was like for some of your favorite stars. Turn the page to check out all the exciting stories and photos of their childhoods. And find out if they really were *just like you*!

Shane Battier

At Duke University, Shane Battier was the perfect student athlete.

"I had the best time of my life in college," Shane said. "I was in no rush to get out there."

Growing up in Birmingham, Michigan, Shane was always interested in things besides sports.

When he was 12 years old, he was the first chair of 106 trumpets at Birmingham's youth orchestra concert.

His senior year, Shane was given the Headmasters Cup as the school's student of the year.

But, he still found plenty of time for basketball. On the court, he led his high-school team to a 93-11 record and three state titles.

Shane was very focused when he came to Duke. But during his time there he learned to relax and enjoy life.

"I was very serious in school. I was serious in basketball," Shane said. "I looked at life as some sort of work to be done."

But that didn't last long. "What I learned at Duke was to laugh at yourself. Laugh often. Smile a lot. All that work would be for nothing if I didn't stop to enjoy it."

And that's just what he did.

He earned his degree and, as a senior, led Duke to the 2001 NCAA Championship. He was the National Player of the Year. Shane is one of only four college players to score more than 1,500 points, 500 rebounds, 200 steals, 200 assists and 200 blocked shots.

And when he graduated, the NBA was waiting. Shane was drafted sixth overall by the Memphis Grizzlies in 2001.

"I work hard to achieve my goals," Shane has said. "If that sets a good example for others to follow, that's great. It seems like everything comes together when you work hard."

Mike Bibby

Maybe Mike Bibby was just born to become a NBA player. After all, his father, Henry, played in the league for almost ten years!

Mike's basketball skills may come from his father, but his mother helped, too. According to Mike, his mother, Virginia, gave him the values and work ethic he needed.

"You know, my mom isn't a famous person like my dad," said Mike. "But she's the reason I'm here. That's who I am."

Mike was born in Cherry Hill, New Jersey, while his father was playing for the Philadelphia 76ers.

Of course, Mike had a long way to go before he could follow in his father's footsteps.

Mike grew up in Phoenix,

Arizona, with his mother, Virginia, brothers Hank and Dane, and sisters Charlsie and Roslyn.

He started playing basketball with his older brothers. He soon became one of the top high-school players in the nation. As a senior at Shadow Mountain High, Mike averaged 34 points per game. He led the team to the state title.

By the time he graduated, Mike was the three-time Arizona High School Player of the Year and set a state high-school scoring record with 3,002 points.

After high school, Mike accepted a scholarship to play at the University of Arizona.

During his freshman year at Arizona, Mike helped Arizona win the 1997 NCAA championship. Mike had 20 points and nine rebounds in the victory over Kentucky.

Mike left Arizona after his sophomore season and was selected number two overall by the Vancouver Grizzlies in the 1998 NBA Draft. He was traded to Sacramento before the 2001–2002 season.

He has only been in the NBA for a few years, but he is already a star.

Jarron and Jason Collins

If you hung around them long enough, you would probably start to notice some slight differences.

Still, Jarron Collins said that if anyone was going to play him in a movie, it would have to be

his brother, Jason. That makes sense, since they look exactly alike.

Jarron and Jason look so much alike that when they were growing up in North Hollywood, California, their teachers would often get them confused.

Sometimes, they could even fool their parents.

"When they were younger, it was difficult," their mother, Portia Collins, said. "But that's when they were really, really young. When they have different haircuts, it's easy. Still, sometimes I do a double take."

Even if people had trouble figuring out who was who, it was always clear that both Jarron and Jason where special people.

When they were infants, the twins modeled baby clothes on a television show. And as teenagers, they appeared in commercials.

Both were honor students at Harvard-Westlake High School.

But they scored their biggest achievements on the court. The twins started playing basketball when they were six years old. Their father taught them how.

And as they started to grow, they kept getting better. By the time they reached high school, the twins were both nearly seven feet tall! They were also both amazing players.

During the summer, Jarron and Jason helped younger kids learn how to play basketball at Michael Jordan's summer camp.

Back in school, they were both named *Parade* magazine All-America basketball players at Harvard-Westlake. They led their team to two state titles.

After graduating from high school, the twins decided to keep playing together. They both accepted scholarships to Stanford University.

They were outstanding

players *and* outstanding students. After their final year at Stanford, their dreams came true. Jason and Jarron were both selected in the 2001 NBA Draft.

Jason was selected in the first round by the Houston Rockets and then traded to the New Jersey Nets. As a rookie, he played against the Los Angeles Lakers in the NBA Finals.

Jarron was selected in the second round by the Utah Jazz, where he plays with legendary players Karl Malone and John Stockton.

Even though the twins are no longer teammates, they both understand how special it is to have their hard work turn into NBA careers.

According to Jarron, there's only one way to make it happen: "Never give up on your dreams."

Baron Davis

When Baron Davis was three years old, his grandfather built him a basketball court. Baron knew his grandfather loved watching him play, so he played on the court all the time.

That was the beginning of a love of basketball that would lead Baron to the NBA.

"When he built my basketball court, that was all I wanted to do, because it came from him." Baron said. "I was going to make him proud."

Baron played and played and played. By the time he got to Crossroads High School, he had become one of the top young players on the West Coast.

Baron, who was named the

California High School Player of the Year, received a scholarship to UCLA.

As a freshman, Baron averaged 15.9 points and 5.1 assists. He was named Pac-10 Freshman of the Year.

When Baron entered the 1999 NBA Draft, he was drafted number three overall by the Charlotte Hornets.

Since becoming a star, Baron has tried his best to help his community. He created a basketball camp for kids, which is something he loved when *he* was a kid.

Baron attended his first camp at Ohio State University when he was a seventh grader in 1992.

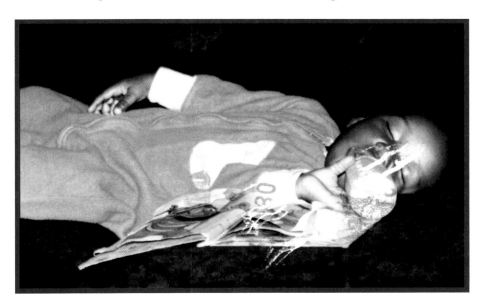

That was also the summer of the Los Angeles riots.

"One of my teachers paid my way to go to camp during the riots," said Baron. "He wanted me to clear my head so I wouldn't be dwelling on the things going on in my neighborhood.

"I told him, 'I owe you,' and he said, 'Just do it for someone else.'" It took Baron a few years, but now he's able to do just what his teacher asked.

Richard Hamilton

Richard "Rip" Hamilton first decided that he wanted to play basketball when he was six years old. His father, Richard, decided that if they were going to do it, they were going to do it right.

So Rip's dad brought a video camera and he started videotaping Rip playing in games, at practice, and dribbling in the driveway.

And when all the chores were completed and the homework was done, father and son would sit down and watch the tape. They studied Rip's game, looking for strengths and weaknesses.

There are now hundreds of videos in Richard Hamilton's collection. They show his son growing from a beginner to a McDonald's

All-American at Coatsville (Pennsylvania) High, to an All-America and NCAA champion at the University of Connecticut, to a budding NBA star with the Detroit Pistons.

"All of those videos are priceless to me," Richard Hamilton said. "You can't put a value on something like that. Those videos represent a family relationship."

Family was the guiding force for Rip when he was growing up in Coatsville, Pennsylvania, just outside of Philadelphia.

While some of the other kids were getting into trouble, Rip was listening to his parents, going to church, going to school, studying and, of course, playing basketball.

Some of the Hamilton's favorite videos show Rip playing in high school

against his good friend — Kobe Bryant.

Rip went on to college at the University of Connecticut, where he won a basketball scholarship.

Before Rip's junior year, his beloved grandfather Edward passed away.

"His death really hit me hard," Rip said. "He was a big influence on me."

Rip went back to the court, determined to make his grandfather proud. He wanted to lead Connecticut to its first NCAA Final Four. Not only did Rip lead UConn to the 1999 Final Four, but he was named MVP as the Huskies upset number one Duke to win the title.

"Grandpop is looking down on you," Richard Hamilton told his son. "You couldn't make him any prouder than what you are doing now."

Rip entered the NBA Draft after his junior season and was selected seventh overall by the Washington Wizards. He pointed to heaven when NBA commissioner David Stern called his name.

"The one thing I wanted to do was give my

Grandpop a little shout," Rip said. "I pointed up there to let everyone know that he is still special in my life."

After two seasons in Washington, he was traded to the Detroit Pistons, where he continues to be one of the top young stars in the league.

His father still collects videos of Rip's games. But now he no longer has to film them himself!

Jarron Collins

Shane Battier

Richard Hamilton

Jamal Mashburn

Baron Davis

Wally Szczerbiak

Mike Bibby

Jason Collins

Jason Kidd

Jason Kidd

A lot of kids grow up dreaming of someday playing against NBA stars.

Jason Kidd didn't have to wait very long.

Even as a kid, Jason was good, but he wasn't the best player on the playgrounds in Oakland, California. That was future NBA star Gary Payton.

Gary was four years older than Jason.

He saw Jason's ability and decided to help.

It wouldn't be easy.

Gary thought the best way to help Jason become a better player was to make sure he could handle himself when the going got tough.

Gary used to shout at Jason, and insult him on the court — he was trying to teach Jason an important lesson.

"I think early on, I was a little intimidated." Jason said. "Now, I know that he was trying to make me a better basketball player, and also a better person. If

somebody is verbal, you don't have to react."

Gary taught Jason plenty of lessons on the court. But there were plenty of things he already knew — he had been playing basketball since third grade!

The first sport Jason loved was soccer, but by third grade, he was hooked on basketball.

Because most of his friends were still playing soccer, Jason would end up playing basketball with older kids. In a lot of those games, Jason wasn't allowed to shoot the ball. So he learned to pass. This kept his teammates happy and always got him invited back.

Jason's passing ability was legendary around Oakland. At St. Joseph of Notre Dame High

School, Jason became the biggest thing since Gary Payton, who had left for college.

Jason led St. Joseph's to two state titles. As a senior, he was given the Naismith Award as the best high-school player in the nation.

Some thought Jason would go straight to the NBA out of high school. But he went to the University of California instead.

Jason played two years at California and then declared himself eligible for the 1994 NBA Draft. He was picked second by the Dallas Mavericks.

"I used to be a little bit tougher on Jason," Gary Payton remembers. "I used to talk to Jason a lot different than the other guys because I knew he was going to be one of the great basketball players."

And Gary was right.

Jamal Mashburn

New York is a big city.

From museums to the theater, from art galleries to basketball courts, it has a lot to offer.

And Jamal Mashburn's mother, Helen, wanted her son to experience all of it.

Even as a kid, Jamal was a great basketball player. But Helen wanted him to know that there was much more to the world than sneakers, a ball, and a hoop.

It was a lesson Jamal never forgot.

"My mother took me to museums all the time when I was younger," said Jamal. "I want to do that for my kids. I want to open them up to different things."

After leading Cardinal Hayes

High to its first New York City Championship since 1944, Jamal won a scholarship to the University of Kentucky.

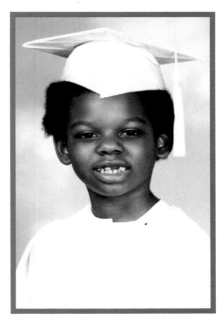

In 1994, Jamal's junior year, he was named an All-American, and the Wildcats went to the Final Four. After that season, he entered the NBA Draft.

Jamal started his career with the Dallas Mavericks and then joined the Miami Heat before being traded to Charlotte. He came with the Hornets when they moved to New Orleans.

While Jamal has enjoyed a long NBA career, he remembers his mother's lesson that basketball isn't the only important thing in life. So he set up a way to help other kids get an education at the University of Kentucky.

Shortly after he signed his first NBA contract, Jamal donated $500,000 to set up the Kentucky Excel Incentive Scholarship Program.

"To me, it's all about giving kids a chance," said Jamal. "When I was growing up, my mom always

told me that without basketball I probably wouldn't get a chance to go to college because it was too expensive.

"There are so many kids out there who need that chance because they don't have sports to fall back on to get them an athletic scholarship. College is so important. Everyone deserves a chance."

Thanks to Jamal, a lot of kids are going to get one.

Wally Szczerbiak

When Wally Szczerbiak decided he wanted to learn basketball, he listened closely to what his father, Walt, told him.

"He always told me, 'Wally, as long as you have fun playing the game, I'll guide you in the right direction and help you out,'" Wally said. "'But there are never guarantees, so just keep having fun with it.'"

Walt Szczerbiak knew all about dreaming of being in the NBA. As a basketball star at George Washington University, he had wanted to make the NBA. But he didn't.

That didn't end Walt's dreams of playing professional basketball.

In 1971, Walt played one season for the Pittsburgh Condors in the old

American Basketball Association. He then moved on to play for Real Madrid of the Spanish League. He still holds the Spanish League record of scoring 65 points in a game.

Wally was born in Madrid in 1977, and he soon learned the game his father loved. His earliest memories are of shooting jump shots with a Nerf ball into a basket on the refrigerator.

The Szczerbiaks, Walt and Marilyn, stayed in Spain until Wally was six years old and then moved to Long Island, New York.

Father and son spent countless hours playing one-on-one in the family's driveway.

"Wally always loved to play," Walt said. "I didn't have to push him."

To make the games more even, Walt would play left-handed and wasn't allowed to block Wally's shots.

Even so, Wally didn't beat his father one-on-one until he was a freshman in college.

All that practice turned Wally into a great player. He starred at Cold Spring Harbor High

School, averaging 36.6 points and 15.9 rebounds in his senior season.

But Cold Spring Harbor isn't a big school, and Wally was overlooked by big colleges. He ended up at Miami University in Ohio.

But he still had his NBA dreams.

In the summer of 1997, Wally went on a strenuous training routine. He lost weight, got stronger, and added four inches to his vertical leap.

In 1998, Wally competed against most of the top college players and made the United States team for the Goodwill Games. Wally was the leading scorer and the United States won the gold medal.

By Wally's senior year at Miami, everyone knew who he was. His outstanding record in the 1999 NCAA Tournament led the Red Hawks to their first ever Sweet 16.

After graduation, Wally fulfilled a dream for both

himself and his father when he was drafted in the lottery by the Minnesota Timberwolves.

"A lot of my dreams have been fulfilled," Wally said, "but I want to keep getting better."

So far, that's exactly what he's doing — and there's no telling how far he'll go.

Guess Who!

Each of these kids grew up to be an NBA superstar. Can you figure out who's who? Turn the page to find the answers.

A.

B.

C

D.

E.

A. Shane Battier

B. Richard Hamilton

C. Baron Davis

D. Mike Bibby

E. Wally Szczerbiak